Novels for Students, Volume 44

Project Editor: Sara Constantakis Rights Acquisition and Management: Sheila Spencer Composition: Evi Abou-El-Seoud Manufacturing: Rhonda Dover

Imaging: John Watkins

Product Design: Pamela A. E. Galbreath, Jennifer Wahi Digital Content Production: Allie Semperger Product Manager: Meggin Condino © 2014 Gale, Cengage Learning

For product information and technology assistance, contact us at **Gale Customer Support, 1-800-877-4253.**

For permission to use material from this text or product, submit all requests online at **www.cengage.com/permissions.**

Further permissions questions can be emailed to **permissionrequest@cengage.com** While every effort has been made to ensure the reliability of the information presented in this publication, Gale, a part of Cengage Learning, does not guarantee the accuracy of the data contained herein. Gale accepts no payment for listing; and inclusion in the publication of any organization, agency, institution, publication, service, or individual does not imply endorsement of the editors or publisher. Errors brought to the attention of the publisher and verified to the satisfaction of the publisher will be corrected in future editions.

Gale
27500 Drake Rd.
Farmington Hills, MI, 48331-3535

ISBN-13: 978-1-4144-9487-6
ISBN-10: 1-4144-9487-4
ISSN 1094-3552

This title is also available as an e-book.

ISBN-13: 978-1-4144-9273-5
ISBN-10: 1-4144-9273-1
Contact your Gale, a part of Cengage Learning sales
representative for ordering information.

Printed in Mexico
1 2 3 4 5 6 7 17 16 15 14 13

The Leopard

Giuseppe di Lampedusa

1959

Introduction

The Leopard (1959), by Giuseppe Tomasi, the prince of Lampedusa, is perhaps the best-known modern Italian novel in the English-speaking world. Produced in a modern Italy that was trying to put the dismal history of Fascism behind it and had been split apart by economic changes after World War II that brought prosperity to the north but left the south in squalid poverty, *The Leopard* is a nostalgic meditation on the nation's past. The novel is closely based on Lampedusa's own family history and is set during the Risorgimento, the unification of Italy that took place around the same time as the American Civil War. Lampedusa's grandfather had been a great landholder in Sicily, but he died without a will, and his fortune was consumed by decades of legal wrangling among his heirs. Lampedusa, the inheritor of not much more than his title, grew up in the shadow of his ancestor's nobility and looked back on it as a lost paradise. In *The Leopard*, he conveys his heartbreaking longing for the world that had been swept away by modernity. For Lampedusa, the loss everyone feels when leaving childhood is magnified into the loss of an entire world.

Author Biography

Giuseppe Tomasi di Lampedusa was born on December 23, 1896, at his ancestral palace in Palermo, Sicily. Technically his surname was Tomasi, and he was the last person to hold the title of Prince of Lampedusa (a tiny island in the Mediterranean between Sicily and Tunisia). The Tomasi family had been members of the European nobility going back to the Middle Ages and had, particularly since the seventeenth century, controlled large estates on Sicily near Palermo. *The Leopard* is very much a reflection on Tomasi family history. Almost every character and event of the novel can be linked to a historical member of the Tomasi family and the details of their lives, but while the novel is in some sense a history, it is one that was transformed to become an artistic creation.

Prince Giulio, Lampedusa's grandfather and the model for Don Fabrizio in the novel, died without a will in 1885, and the subsequent division of his estate among his heirs, involving decades of legal battles, left the Tomasi family in a relatively diminished and impoverished position. Lampedusa fought in World War I and was captured by the Austrians, but he managed to escape from a prison camp in Hungary and return to Italy. Disgusted by the rise of the Fascist government in Italy, he devoted himself to the study of foreign literature and spent much of his life in London, where he met his wife, Alexandra Wolff von Stomersee, the daughter of the Latvian consul. They were married in 1932 but had to live much of their lives apart because of the tyrannical influence of Lampedusa's mother. During World War II, the Lampedusa palace in Palermo was destroyed by American bombing.

After the war, Lampedusa's wife became one of the leading psychoanalysts in Italy. She encouraged her husband to write memoirs exploring his childhood and early life. These eventually became the basis of *The Leopard*. The earliest version of these writings, *Places of My Infancy*, has also been translated into English and was published in the collection *Two Stories and a Memory*. Lampedusa became attached to a circle of young intellectuals and writers in Rome, Italy, which included his cousin, the poet Luccio Piccolo, whom Lampedusa adopted. Lampedusa delivered lectures to this group on French and English literature; the text of these lectures has been published but not translated. *The Leopard* was rejected by several publishers during Lampedusa's lifetime because of its reactionary nature. Lampedusa died of lung cancer on July 23, 1957, in Rome. The manuscript of *The Leopard* circulated among Lampedusa's friends. It was finally published in 1959 and translated into English the following year.

Plot Summary

The Leopard is the translation of the Italian title *Il gattopardo*. However, the Italian word actually refers to a serval, a type of small spotted cat that was native to Sicily but that became extinct there in the middle of the nineteenth century. The serval, rather than the leopard, was the heraldic animal of the princes of Lampedusa, as it is of the princes of Salina in the novel.

Introduction to the Prince (May 1860)

The Leopard begins during the invasion of Sicily by Giuseppe Garibaldi and his thousand volunteers. This invasion sparks a civil war in the kingdom of the two Sicilies, leading to the unification of Italy into a single modern state under the ruling house of Piedmont from northern Italy.

The novel begins in the Salina palace in Palermo as the prince, Don Fabrizio, and his family are being led in saying the rosary by their chaplain, Father Pirrone. Afterward, the prince walks in his garden with his dog, Benedico. He recalls the dismembered body of a Neapolitan soldier that was recently found there, killed by Garibaldi's "Redshirt" soldiers, who are massing in the hills above the city. That night, the prince visits his mistress in the city. He takes Father Pirrone with him so that he can visit the Jesuit house in town, where he learns how alarmed the Church authorities are about the invasion and uprising. Don Fabrizio spends his days doing astronomical work (he is a prominent amateur astronomer) and in looking after the affairs of his estate, particularly in meetings with his accountant, Ciccio Ferrara, and his chief agent, Pietro Russo. These scenes give the prince scope to express his disgust with the rising middle class who are going to be propelled into power by the coming revolution, but also his helplessness in the face of the future. His beloved nephew, Tancredi, and Russo are both are secretly allied with the building revolution. Tancredi visits his uncle and explains to him that change is inevitable and that he must join the revolution in order to guide it in a way that will protect the family's way of life. In fact, Tancredi is going to openly join Garibaldi's army. The prince thinks about the contrasts between Tancredi and his own eldest son and heir, Paolo, whom he considers ineffectual and boorish, and his favorite son, Giovanni, who has run away to England to find freedom in making a life for himself without depending on his father's influence. The prince receives an anonymous letter advising his family to go to his country estate of Donnafugata, where they will be safe.

Media Adaptations

- *The Leopard* was filmed by Luchino Visconti in 1963, staring the American actor Burt Lancaster as Don Fabrizio. The film won the Palme d'Or at the Cannes Film Festival. While European audiences saw a version in Italian with Lancaster's lines dubbed, the American release used Lancaster's voice and dubbed the other actors into English. The American version was also shorter by twenty-four minutes. The recent Criterion Collection DVD release contains both the full (subtitled) and edited versions

Donnafugata (August 1860)

Once in his country palace outside the small town of Donnafugata, the prince learns that Calogero Sedàra, the local mayor, had been quick to ally himself with the Redshirts and has amassed a large fortune, nearly equal to the prince's own, through sharp business dealings, usually at the expense of aristocrats. Father Pirrone brings Don Fabrizio a message from his daughter Concetta: she is in love with Tancredi and believes that he is on the verge of proposing to her, and she wants to know how her father wishes her to answer. But the prince does not give a definite answer. Sedàra and other prominent commoners are invited to dinner at the palace that evening. Sedaòra brings his daughter Angelica, who is remarkably beautiful and who sets her romantic sights on Tancredi. Father Pirrone retreats from her erotic allure and takes refuge in the Bible, but he reads the stories of Delilah, Judith, and Esther, all women who used their feminine wiles to bring about the downfall of men. Tancredi tells stories of his adventures in the recent war (now over in Sicily, but continuing on the mainland), including a raid on a convent. Concetta finds this outrageous and takes personal offense. The next day, Tancredi takes up the same line, when the family makes a visit to a convent of which the prince is the patron, and she reacts just as strongly. Thereafter, Tancredi begins courting Angelica.

The Troubles of Don Fabrizio

(October 1860)

Fabrizio grows dissatisfied with his diminished role in the new world created by the revolution. Tancredi is back with Garibaldi's army at the siege of Gaeta, but he continues his courtship of Angelica through letters. She is a daily visitor at the palace. While Fabrizio is out hunting with his friend Ciccio Tumeo, the church organist, Fabrizio discusses the recent vote on whether Sicily should join the Kingdom of Piedmont and move toward Italian unification. The prince had voted yes, but Ciccio had voted against it, clinging to his traditional loyalties. Yet the election results from Donnafugata, certified by Sedàra, had supposedly been unanimously in favor. Both men are appalled that the election has been falsified, and they realize that it exposes the utopian promises of the new régime as false. Ciccio starts to speak against Sedàra, but the prince stops him, telling him the man is soon to become Tancredi's father-in-law and must be respected. This deeply shocks Ciccio, who had thought that Tancredi was only trying to seduce Angelica in order to humiliate her father, Sedàra.

In a meeting with Sedàra, Fabrizio arranges the marriage of Tancredi and Angelica. They realize that whatever their feelings, they need each other. The Salina family needs Sedàra's wealth for Tancredi, and Sedàra needs the Salina connection for prestige.

Love at Donnafugata (November

1860)

Tancredi, now commissioned in the royal army of Piedmont, visits Donnafugata and spends blissful days with Angelica, showing her the estate and introducing her to the family traditions. Although the novel reveals little of their married life together, the narrative voice remarks on the contrast between this time of happiness and their future, miserable married life. Don Fabrizio is visited by Aimone Chevalley di Monterzuolo, a representative of the Piedmontese crown, who is there to offer him the position of senator. But the prince refuses, realizing that he has no place in the new world that is being created around him. The next day the prince sees the emissary off at the train station, and they observe the poverty that oppresses the lives of the peasants in Donnafugata. They would both like to see it change; Monterzuolo believes that it will, while the prince believes that it cannot.

Father Pirrone Pays a Visit (February 1861)

This chapter is a digression from the plot of the novel and is nearly a stand-alone short story. Father Pirrone visits his home village. He finds that the land rented by the local peasants had been transferred from the nearby Benedictine monastery to a peasant moneylender, considerably worsening the peasants' economic rights and position. He comes to believe that the nobles like his patron Don Fabrizio are doing nothing to correct these evils because they live in a world apart and have no practical understanding of what is happening. He becomes involved in a marriage matter that is a mirror reflection of that between Angelica and Tancredi. His own niece has become pregnant out of wedlock, and he arranges a marriage with the father, which also ends an age-old feud between the two peasant families involved. However, this had all been carefully planned by the other family to seize the priest's brother's property as a dowry.

A Ball (November 1862)

Back in Palermo, the Salina family attends a ball that is the highlight of the social calendar of the city's nobility. It will be Angelica's presentation to noble society. At the ball, Fabrizio realizes that not only is his youth over but the very way of life he grew up in is gone. The other aristocrats at the ball seem to him like so many inbred pygmies, the motions of their dance like the circling of crows over a corpse. Seeing Angelica and Tancredi dance, he realizes that theirs is a union of greed and ambition, but he cannot help but love them. The ball lasts until dawn, and the prince walks home while his family goes ahead in their carriages. He observes a cartload of slaughtered bulls, a symbol of the death of the Italian nobility, and contrasts it with the unchanging beauty of the heavens, particularly the planet Venus, which, still visible, fills him with a sense of joy.

Death of a Prince (July 1888)

Twenty-six years after the last chapter, Don Fabrizio is dying. He and his family are returning to Sicily by train from a visit to a specialist physician in Naples. Tancredi is rising in the government, and the prince's heir, Paolo, has died in a riding accident, leaving the prince's grandson Fabrizetto as his heir, but Fabrizio likes him no better than he had Paolo. His son Giovanni has become a successful diamond merchant, and his wife has died years ago. Unable to quite make it back to his own palace, the prince dies of a stroke in a hotel in Palermo, realizing that a whole older world is passing away with him. A mysterious female apparition, perhaps the embodiment of his earlier vision of the planet Venus, conducts him to the next world.

Relics (May 1910)

Twenty-two years later, the Salina palace at Palermo is now occupied by Concetta and two of her sisters, none of whom ever married. They have devoted themselves to religion and amassed a large collection of relics, which are undergoing an examination for authenticity by Church officials, who eventually reject most of them. Tancredi has died, but the sisters are still close to Angelica, who uses her wealth and influence to control politics on the island. She visits them and promises to keep the potentially scandalous exposure of their relics quiet. She brings with her Senator Tassoni, an old friend of Tancredi's from their days with Garibaldi, who wishes to meet the remaining members of his comrade's family. Tancredi had often told him of Concetta. He reveals that Tancredi had indeed intended to marry her, and the story of violating the monastery had been a fiction, meant as a joking allusion to Tancredi's desire to conquer his cousin's chastity, but her rejection had made the situation impossible, so he had transferred his attention to another for political advantage. The immense weight of the misery of Angelica's life, which she had unintentionally and unknowingly inflicted upon herself, crushes down on her, but she also realizes that it is useless to indulge in this pain that will consume her. She orders the taxidermied body of the prince's dog Benedico destroyed; it is the last relic of her father.

Angelina

Angelina is the niece of Father Pirrone. His two brothers had long been feuding over a disputed land inheritance, and Angelina's uncle had arranged for his son to seduce her so as to force a marriage and bring the land back into his line of the family as a dowry. This is meant as a distorted reflection of the marriage arrangements first between Tancredi and Concetta and then of Tancredi and Angelica. (Angelina is a diminutive form of Angelica.) The affair causes Father Pirrone to reflect that peasants and nobles have the same ambitions and purposes, only on different scales.

Concetta Corbera

Concetta is the daughter of Don Fabrizio. The family expected that she would marry her cousin Tancredi, but she makes this impossible when she misunderstands a joke of Tancredi's that was actually intended to compliment her. She had been in love with him, and the rest of her life is spent in misery because of this romantic failure. The waste of her life competes with the general fall of the nobility that so concerns Fabrizio as the tragedy of the novel. She had imagined her whole life that Tancredi had purposefully outraged her by uttering what she considered blasphemy and hence had never loved her. The truth is revealed to her only at the end of the novel by one of Tancredi's friends who happens to visit her, plunging her into deeper despair than she had already known.

Fabrizietto Corbera

The prince's grandson has the same name and eventually the same titles as his grandfather, but he is called by the diminutive Fabrizietto. Don Fabrizio holds him in the same contempt he did his father, in particular because he adopts middle-class ways.

Don Fabrizio Corbera, Prince of Salina

From the beginning of the novel, Fabrizio is described in terms more godlike than human: "his huge frame made the floor tremble, and a glint of pride flashed in his light blue eyes at this fleeting confirmation of his lordship over both human beings and their works." He is "very large and strong; in houses inhabited by lesser mortals his head would touch the lowest rosette on the chandeliers; his fingers could twist a ducat coin as if it were mere paper.... But those fingers could also stoke and handle with the most exquisite delicacy." His mother, Princess Carolina, had come from Germany, and the prince is fair-skinned and blonde. He also has other Germanic characteristics that are seen as out of place in Sicily: "an authoritarian temperament, a certain rigidity in morals, and a propensity for abstract ideas; these, in the relaxing atmosphere of Palermo society, had changed respectively into capricious arrogance, recurring moral scruples, and contempt for his own relatives and friends, all of whom seemed to him mere driftwood in the languid meandering stream of Sicilian pragmatism." The narrative of the novel grows out of Fabrizio's habit of introspection, or thoughtfulness. The depth of his character and of his consciousness of class and place is the true subject of *The Leopard*. Don Fabrizio is the last link in the chain of noble tradition, a fact that makes him tower over his modern contemporaries. But at the same time, his isolation from political and economic affairs makes him powerless to control his own fate or halt the decline he sees everywhere around him. He eventually becomes dependent on bourgeois (middle-class, as opposed to aristocratic) culture in the form of Sedaòra, the rich peasant mayor of Donnafugata, and even of his nephew Tancredi, who must become a politician in order to carry on the family's prestige, albeit in a form that is altered and diminished.

Francesco Paolo Corbera

His father considers him a "booby" compared with his favored nephew, Tancredi, and he is of minor importance as a character. He eventually dies in a riding accident.

Giovanni Corbera

Giovanni is Don Fabrizio's second son. Before the action of the novel, he had run away to England and taken up work as a lowly clerk, preferring his independence to being kept, as he saw it, almost as a pet in Sicily. Although he is the only child to physically resemble his father, he never returns to the family. He eventually finds success as a diamond merchant.

Maria Stella Corbera, Princess of Salina

Maria Stella is Don Fabrizio's wife. Maria, "restless and domineering," is a mystery to her husband. He complains that despite having several children with her, he has never seen her navel, but clearly has little interest in her as a companion or even as a human being. The narrative of the book presents her in a somewhat hysterical manner, as when "her fine crazy eyes glanced around at her slaves of children and her tyrant of a husband." She superstitiously believes, her husband notes, that comets are an ill omen. To Fabrizio the astronomer this is, of course, ridiculous. But it is also an indication of the gulf that separates them. They live in different worlds and he cannot even imagine trying to communicate with her. She eventually dies of diabetes, which could not be treated in the nineteenth century.

Angelica Falconeri (née Sedàra)

Though of a lower class, Angelica is able to marry into the prince's family because she brings much-needed wealth for the advancement of her husband Tancredi's political career. She is possessed of remarkable natural beauty and considerable intelligence, and Tancredi is able to train her in aristocratic manners so that she can be accepted in the highest circles without reserve. However, her character, hidden under a beautiful surface, remains essentially identical to that of her scheming, bourgeois father. She is shown as incapable of refined, genuine emotion: "Anyone deducing ... that [Angelica] loved Tancredi would have been mistaken; she had too much pride and too much ambition to be capable of that annihilation, however temporary, of one's own personality without which there is no love." Ultimately she echoes her father's drives for power and control: "years later, she became one of the most venomous string pullers for Parliament and Senate."

Tancredi Falconeri

Tancredi is Don Fabrizio's beloved nephew, the son of his favorite sister, whom he looks on as his spiritual, if not his legal, heir: "Though the Prince never admitted it to himself, he would have preferred the lad as his heir to that booby Paolo." Nevertheless, Tancredi is deeply involved with liberal causes and eventually joins Garibaldi's army. Since *The Leopard* is told from the prince's perspective, much of Tancredi's importance in the novel comes from his relationship to his uncle.

Tancredi "had become very dear to the irascible Prince, who perceived in him a riotous zest for life and a frivolous temperament contradicted by sudden serious moods." In other words, the prince saw his own character in his nephew. Tancredi is not betraying his class or family, however, as he realizes the only way to protect his interests is by controlling the course of the revolution from within. He therefore forges an alliance with the rising bourgeois class through his marriage to the heiress Angelica. Fabrizio at first excuses his nephew's immersion in the modern world of liberal politics —"Tancredi could never do wrong in his uncle's eyes"—but eventually comes to see that Tancredi acted in the best interests of his social class, even though his victories against the tide of revolution and modernization are limited.

Don Ciccio Ferrara

Ciccio is the prince's accountant. As indicated by the honorific *Don*, Ciccio is of a little higher social status than most of Fabrizio's servants. Nevertheless, to the prince, "he was a scraggy little man who hid the deluded and rapacious mind of a 'liberal' behind reassuring spectacles and immaculate cravats." To the prince, Ciccio seems to miss the essential qualities of the world around him and replace them with a sort of fictitious drama that describes only its surface. When he is through working with Ciccio and the concerns of the modern world he represents, Fabrizio feels he is "soaring back through the clouds."

Aimone Chevalley di Monterzuolo

Monterzuolo is a representative of the Piedmontese government. He journeys to Donnafugata to offer Don Fabrizio a place in the new government as a senator. His attitude favoring technology and modernization is in contrast with the prince's acceptance of tradition.

Father Pirrone

Pirrone is a Jesuit priest. As was normal for an aristocratic family in the old tradition, Don Fabrizio employs a priest to act as the family confessor and to lead them in their spiritual lives. But Pirrone is also a trained mathematician; he is Fabrizio's calculator (a term originally applied to human beings who carried out difficult computations) and assists him in his astronomical work. The narrator sometimes takes Pirrone's point of view to offer a more objective picture of events.

Pietro Russo

Russo is Don Fabrizio's chief manager of his extensive estates. With his traditional feelings about class, Fabrizio thinks of him as "some red-skinned peasant, which is what that name of [his] means." Yet Fabrizio is forced by circumstance to also form a very different opinion of Russo: "Clever, dressed rather smartly in a striped velvet jacket, with greedy eyes below a remorseless forehead, the Prince found him a perfect specimen of a class on its way up."

Though he does not openly admit it, Russo is deeply involved in the revolutionary movement sweeping through Sicily and will presently gain political influence once it succeeds. Fabrizio is distressed by people like Russo because all they want is wealth, and in the future that wealth will give them a status approaching his own. To them, aristocratic lineage and airs are things they can acquire, not an essential part of themselves.

Calogero Sedàra

Sedàra is a bourgeois businessman who has accumulated vast wealth and the outward appearance of respectability by becoming the mayor of Donnafugata (hence his title of *Don*) but whose manners still mark him as a peasant who appears clownish to the prince: "Don Fabrizio found an odd admiration growing in him for Sedàra's qualities. He became used to the ill-shaven cheeks, the plebeian accent, the odd clothes, and the persistent odor of stale sweat, and he began to realize the man's rare intelligence." Once the marriage is set between Angelica and Tancredi, Sedàra uses his business experience to make himself useful to the prince, though only in ways that are contrary to Fabrizio's whole philosophy of life: "Problems that had seemed insoluble to the Prince were resolved in a trice by Don Calogero; free as he was from the shackles imposed on many other men by honesty, decency, and plain good manners, he moved through the jungle of life with the confidence of an elephant which advances in a straight line."

Although contact with this representative of the modern world seems immediately helpful to the prince, it will ultimately destroy the Salina family: "Don Calogero's advice … was both opportune and immediately effective; but the eventual result of such advice, cruelly efficient … was that in years to come the Salina family were to acquire a reputation for treating dependents harshly,… without in any way halting the collapse of the family fortunes." Even while Sedaòra remains the prince's dependent, the prince also becomes paradoxically dependent on Sedàra to maintain his own position in the new order of society, leaving him feeling lost and defeated.

Senator Tassoni

Tassoni is an old friend of Tancredi from his days in the Redshirts. He was also briefly Angelica's lover. In her old age his passing mention of Tancredi reveals to her that she had missed her chance of marrying her cousin.

Ciccio Tumeo

Tumeo is the organist in the church at Donnafugata and the prince's companion in hunting. Despite their class difference, a genuine friendship exists between the two men. Tumeo feels betrayed by Sedàra's fixing of the new election, considering that the new, more nearly republican form of government is falsified by the mere pretense that power is, just as before, really held in a few hands at the top.

Themes

Politics

The Leopard was rejected by several publishers during Lampedusa's lifetime because it seemed unpublishable from a political viewpoint. And, indeed, when it was published after the author's death, at the beginning of the turbulent 1960s, *The Leopard* was attacked from both sides. It was attacked from the left for its seeming celebration of the aristocracy and its attacks on peasants, workers, and even the middle class, and from the right for its portrayal of the same aristocratic class as decadent, corrupt, and impotent. But the fact is, Lampedusa (like his main character Don Fabrizio) is not very interested in politics but rather in the position of his own family. As he is dying, Don Fabrizio reflects:

> For the significance of a noble family lies entirely in its traditions, that is in its vital memories; and he was the last to have any unusual memories, anything different from those of other families.... The last Salina was himself. That fellow Garibaldi, that bearded Vulcan, had won after all.

The tragedy is not the end of old Italy but the end of the Salinas. Those around Fabrizio who hold conservative views express a conventional support for the monarchy: "For the King, who stands for order, continuity, decency, honor, right; for the King, who is sole defender of the Church; sole bulwark against the dispersal of property, 'The Sect's' ultimate aim."("The Sect" means the Freemasons, which in nineteenth-century Italy was a caricature of any force opposed by conservatives, just as the labels *Socialist* and *Communist* have become in modern American politics.) But Fabrizio does not share these views. From before the time of the novel's opening, Don Fabrizio has realized that the Kingdom of the Two Sicilies is doomed because of the crown's incompetence. The only question is whether it would be replaced with a new, more vigorous monarchy (from Piedmont) or whether the monarchic system would collapse entirely into a republic, which would do away with the crown, the aristocracy, and probably his personal fortune.

Certainly Lampedusa's views cannot be confused with the reactionary politics of his own lifetime in Fascist Italy. Lampedusa hated the Fascists, since under Fascism real power lies with the industrial class, which rules with the consent of a public beguiled by a right-wing vision of an ideal past very different from any historical reality and very different from the one held dear by Don Fabrizio. Don Fabrizio's witness to a government of the newly rich who manipulate the peasants is Lampedusa's criticism of Fascism, not of liberalism. Lampedusa breaks out of his historical framework to speak quite openly of his own times: "No one mentions red shirts anymore; but they'll be back.

When they've vanished, others of different colors will come; and then the red ones again. And how will it end?" While he begins with Garibaldi's Redshirts, he clearly moves on to the Fascist Blackshirts, while the return of the Redshirts expresses his concerns over the growth of the Italian Communist Party during the 1950s.

Topics for Further Study

- In the late nineteenth century, traditional Japanese culture was faced with the modern world and chose to modernize, in an era known as the Meiji restoration. There was a terrible social cost in terms of civil war and the eradication of a traditional, aristocratic way of life. The Japanese experience was similar to that of Italy at roughly the same time, although the disruption and transformation of culture was even more profound in the East. Alan Gratz's 2008 book *Samurai Shortstop* is a young-adult novel set in Meiji Japan. It tells the story of a teenage boy from an aristocratic family who witnessed his grandfather commit ritual suicide rather than change with the times. He finds, though, that the modern game of baseball is seemingly the only way he has to fit into the culture of his aristocratic boarding school, as well as the only field in which he can apply the training in the samurai ways he receives from his father. Comparing this novel with *The Leopard*, write your own story from the viewpoint of one of Don Fabrizio's teenage sons. How might his feelings about the relationship of the past and the present be different from his father's?

- *The Leopard* takes place in the early 1860s against the historical backdrop of the Risorgimento, the political and military crisis that resulted in the unification of Italy. At the same time, the United States experienced the Civil War, a conflict between the economically disadvantaged, agricultural South and the industrialized, bourgeois North over the issue of national unity. Write a paper comparing the two conflicts, if possible with reference to the history of your own family during the Civil War.

- Tour companies in Sicily frequently use the popularity of *The Leopard* to promote their business and offer tour packages based on the places described in the novel. Consequently, *The Leopard* is frequently mentioned in blogs kept by tourists. Make a survey of these sites using Internet searches and especially searches of blogs. How does Lampedusa's nostalgia interact with the tourist experience? Write a paper explaining your conclusions.

- Many secondary works devoted to *The Leopard* are illustrated with photographs either from the Lampedusa family archives or of the buildings and places described in the book. Using these and any other sources that are available to you, make a presentation to your class showing images of the world described in *The Leopard*.

Past

The Leopard is an undoubted masterpiece, not so much in its evocation of the past as in its evocation of longing for the past. Don Fabrizio is sure on his deathbed that despite all his efforts, the modern world has swept away the old world that he knew. This means in turn that as the author, Lampedusa feels separated from the past by modernity, which he considers a catastrophe. Fabrizio's nephew Tancredi famously reassures his uncle, "Unless we ourselves take a hand now, they'll foist a republic on us. If we want things to stay as they are, things will have to change." But things change and do not stay as they are, and as the crisis of modernity becomes more acute throughout Lampedusa's lifetime in the two world wars, the republic and the end of the princes of Lampedusa/Salina finally comes. The situation is shown allegorically when, early in the novel, the prince's family is served a dessert pudding that had been sculpted into the shape of a city. By the time it is served to Paolo, the prince's heir, "it consisted only of shattered walls and hunks of wobbly rubble." Like modernity, in T. S. Eliot's phrase in *The Wasteland*, it has become a heap of broken ruins. This foreshadows the state of Don Fabrizio's world when it is left to his descendants.

The Leopard is such a personal exploration that it is difficult to associate it with any particular philosophy (just as it is difficult to associate it with any political movement). In one sense it is an intensely political novel. But in another way, it is clear that the author has a marked distaste for politics. Strictly speaking, the politics of *The Leopard* are reactionary—that is, a conservative reaction against change. This is why Lampedusa could not find a publisher in his lifetime. But the novel was also a favorite of the surrealists, who, politically, were allied with the Communists. Yet there is one political philosophy with which *The Leopard* seems to have some affinities: traditionalism. Although this term has a vast range of meanings, it is in a narrow sense a political movement (as described in Mark Sedgwick's *Against the Modern World: Traditionalism and the Secret Intellectual History of the Twentieth Century*). Traditionalism divides the past into two successive ages. During some golden age in the past, human life existed as an integrated whole full of wisdom and purpose. At some point human life was struck by a disaster that traditionalists refer to as modernity (and depending on the particular version of traditionalism, this can be as late as the Enlightenment or as early as the birth of Christianity or even the Iron Age), and life became a sordid affair stripped of all meaning and significance. Unlike other ideologies with a similar view of history, such as Marxism, traditionalism pointedly offers no solution to the problem it poses, except to patiently wait for the cycles of history to restore the significance that had been lost.

This philosophical view of history does have some correspondence to *The Leopard*: its hero, the introspective but creative and vigorous Don Fabrizio, who represents the humanity of the traditionalist golden age, is nevertheless helpless before the onslaught of modernity as it destroys the traditional world of which he feels himself a part. Traditionalism began in the 1920s in France, with the work of René Guénon, who saw a greater continuity with the traditional world in Islam than in Christian Europe; he eventually moved to Egypt and converted to Sufi Islam. In Italy, traditionalism was represented by Julius Evola, whose private spirituality centered on the practice of ceremonial magic. Lampedusa is not known to have had any contact with Evola, and traditionalists do not claim Lampedusa as one of their own, despite the at least superficial similarity of their ideas. The Nazi Party was founded by the traditionalist Rudolf von Sebottendorf, but Adolf Hitler's seizure of control in the party completely transformed its nature, and von Sebottendorf ended up in a concentration camp. Evola tried to exert influence over Italian Fascism, but his opposition to Christianity caused his writings to be censored by the government of Benito Mussolini. Traditionalism is a fringe movement, but traditionalist groups were responsible for a number of terrorist attacks in Italy throughout the 1960s. The prominent Romanian historian of religion Mircea Eliade was perhaps the best-known traditionalist because of his prominence in the scholarly community. Today, traditionalist parties are able to elect members of parliament in Greece and Russia.

Symbolism

One reason for the initial cool reception of *The Leopard* by publishers was its defiance of modern literary trends, and even of accepted genre categories. The novel is unrelated to the neo-realism that dominated Italian literature during the 1950s (comparable to the journalistic style familiar from well-known films like *Open City* and *The Bicycle Thieves*), and it is related still less to the avant-garde literature of the time. Its outward form is an old-fashioned nineteenth-century historical novel, so its surface narrative is sometimes compared to Margaret Mitchell's *Gone with the Wind.* However, one feature of *The Leopard* is that it is assembled from or uses elements from many styles that were current in the late nineteenth century, around the time of Lampedusa's birth. One of these is symbolism, a French school of literature whose best-known exponent was Paul Verlaine. Symbolism refers to the rejection of the prevailing realism of nineteenth-century French literature and the production of literature with fantastic elements incorporated into the text as if they were real in a manner calculated to reveal an important psychological truth. Symbolist elements in *The Leopard* include the repeated description of figures in paintings, particularly of the pagan gods, as if they were actual characters, as well as the description of Don Fabrizio in superhuman terms. Both techniques are meant to stress that Fabrizio is a relic from an older, greater age. Similarly, when Fabrizio nears death, he sees a young woman on the train platform when he is traveling back home to Palermo from Naples where he had gone to see a specialist. The next day, as he is actually dying in a hotel, the same woman appears in his room among the crowd of his family and doctors. He recognizes her also as a vision he had seen in the stars, and then he dies. This is the intrusion into the narrative of the ancient myth of the valkyrie taking the dead hero to the afterlife. It signifies that the death of the prince is the end of a heroic age.

Decadence

Another style of late-nineteenth-century French literature that Lampedusa intrudes here and there into *The Leopard* is decadence, a movement represented in English in the works of Oscar Wilde. One element of decadence is the close association of the grotesque and the beautiful, and particularly the reconceptualization of the grotesque as the beautiful. Many passages of *The Leopard* are decadent in this sense, for instance, the description of the transformation of the brutality of medieval feudalism into a rare cultivated beauty:

> The wealth of many centuries had been transmitted into ornament, luxury, pleasure; no more; the abolition of feudal rights had swept

away duties as well as privileges; wealth, like an old wine, had let the dregs of greed, even of care and prudence, fall to the bottom of the barrel, leaving only verve and color. And thus eventually it cancelled itself out; this wealth which had achieved its object was composed now only of essential oils—and like essential oils, it soon evaporated.

Most typical of decadence is the connection drawn between sex and death. While driving though an orange grove on his way to visit his mistress, Don Fabrizio inhales "that Islamic perfume evoking houris and fleshly joys beyond the grave." A repeated symbol in *The Leopard*, expressing the depth of the tragedy involved in the loss of the prince's world to modernity, is the image of a mutilated corpse. This occurs first in the dead Neapolitan soldier found in the prince's garden in Palermo with "a pile of purplish intestines [that] had formed a puddle under his bandoleer." The image constantly reasserts itself to the prince's mind:

But the image of that gutted corpse often recurred, as if asking to be given peace in the only possible way the Prince could give it: by justifying that last agony on grounds of general necessity.

And it recurs finally after the ball in Palermo that is effectively the death of the prince's world and the beginning of Tancredi's, as the prince walks back to his palace and sees a vehicle on the road:

> A long open wagon came by stacked with bulls killed shortly before at the slaughter house, already quartered and exhibiting their intimate mechanism with the shamelessness of death. At intervals a big thick red drop fell onto the pavement.

Compare & Contrast

- **1860s:** Italy is a patchwork of independent states, ruled either by hereditary monarchies or by the papacy (government headed by the pope).

  Today: Italy is a unified republic with no monarchic head of state. While the papacy remains politically independent, it is limited to a few acres (Vatican City), inside the city of Rome.

- **1860s:** Marriages at all levels of society are commonly arranged by parents or prominent relatives on the basis of family interest.

  Today: Marriage is essentially a private concern of the couple involved, and its impact on their families is a secondary consideration.

- **1860s:** Wealth was generally produced by agriculture, so there was no practical way to increase it. Thus, one class could rise economically only at the expense of another.
  Today: Wealth is generated by an industrial and postindustrial economy (although southern Italy remains economically disadvantaged compared with the north), and can be generally increased without a fixed limit.

In both cases the sign of death is, unexpectedly, its bright coloration.

The Risorgimento

During the French Revolution, France occupied northern Italy and reorganized its many medieval city-states into the Cisalpine Republic and then, under Napoleon, the Kingdom of Italy. This unification was reversed with the restoration in 1815, and Austria became the overlord of the many small Italian states. However, the Kingdom of Piedmont (or Sardinia) kept the idea of Italian unification alive and by 1860 had unified under its control most of Italy except for the Papal States, the Veneto (directly controlled by Austria), and the Kingdom of Naples (or the Two Sicilies) in the south. Giuseppe Garibaldi had acted as a military leader in many of the wars fought against France and Austria to achieve the goal of Italian unity, sometimes as a commander for Piedmont and sometimes on behalf of schemes to create an Italian republic in cooperation with the political revolutionary Giuseppe Mazzini. Garibaldi, however, was more important as an inspiring leader of the Risorgimento (or "Resurgence") than as an effective military commander.

In 1860, however, Garibaldi was starting to agitate against Piedmont, which had ceded his home town of Nice to France. So the Piedmontese king Victor Emmanuel II and Prime Minister Camillo

Cavour redirected Garibaldi by sending him to Sicily to join a revolt there against the Bourbon monarchy. He landed in Marsala with his volunteer corps, known as the thousand because of their small number and as the Redshirts because of their uniform. They soon succeeded in raising a general rebellion in Sicily, driving out the Bourbon troops, and invading the mainland of Naples. The young King Francis retreated to the fortress of Gaeta, which Garibaldi's irregular army lacked the artillery and equipment to assault. However, the Piedmontese finally sent a regular army through the Papal States and forced Gaeta to surrender in March of 1861. Shortly thereafter Victor Immanuel was declared king of Italy, which was unified except for the city of Rome and Austrian-occupied Venetia. These territories would be added by 1870.

The military and political revolutions that unified Italy also transformed Italian society, increasing the power of the bourgeoisie, or middle class, at the expense of the nobility and spreading ideals of equality and republican government. In *The Leopard*, the prince's nephew Tancredi joins Garibaldi's Redshirts shortly after their landing because he realizes the only way to preserve the prestige of the Salina family is to make it an important factor in the new bourgeois Italy that is coming into existence. The novel explores the tendency of the new political arrangements to inevitably weaken the nobility at the expense of wealthy merchants and industrialists, whatever lip service was at first paid to the aristocracy. The social structure was changed by Italy's entrance into the modern world in economic and political terms, so that the way of life idealized by the aristocracy quickly vanished, leaving only a memory for the prince of Lampedusa to cherish.

Critical Overview

The first few chapters of David Gilmour's *The Last Leopard: A Life of Giuseppe di Lampedusa* sketch the history of the Tomasi family back to the sixteenth century, as far as it can reliably be traced, and draw comparisons between the historical reality and its fictional shadow in *The Leopard*. Gilmour finds the main point of *The Leopard* is the care of Lampedusa for his spiritual inheritance, the only thing he receives after the financial and political decline of his family. Correspondingly, this is the only inheritance that the fictionalized Don Fabrizio is concerned about leaving, but for which he finds no heir. Gilmour's researches in the Lampedusa family archives found that the real Prince Giulio, the model for Don Fabrizio, was a far more insignificant person than Fabrizio is in Lampedusa's idealization of his idea of family.

Initial reaction to *The Leopard* was generally negative (despite the book's rapid rise as an international best seller), with Socialist reviewers attacking Lampedusa's classism and conservatives attacking his anticlericalism and his portrayal of the aristocracy as decadent and impotent. Louis Aragon, however, a surrealist and a Communist, unexpectedly hailed it as one of the greatest novels ever written. American reviews, far removed from European politics, were more positive, even if more innocent, on the book's purely literary merits. Vivian Mercier gave a very favorable notice in the

Hudson Review: "The old order is revealed, even while it is collapsing, as a beautiful thing, a genuine *order*. One almost wishes that the Prince of Salina had fought to preserve it."

An early study of *The Leopard*, Arthur and Catherine Evans's 1963 article in *Wisconsin Studies in Contemporary Literature*, establishes that the novel is not actually historical but is devoted to a particular response to history: "Lampedusa's novel is an analysis of the moral response to change on the part of a man, his class, and his country." The author is in love with a world that is dead, the authors find, so that, "fear, inertia, and pride paralyse land and people in a common death-urge." In their view, Don Fabrizio is desperately trying to maintain his position: "The Prince's response is a wasting fretfulness, a yearning for permanence guaranteed, so he hopes, at the price of compromise and a leonine disdain for others' happiness." The Evanses realize that much of the meaning of the novel is repeated over and over in different symbolic forms. Concentrating on the animal theme of *The Leopard*, they compare the decline from lion to hyena as a metaphor for the rulers whom Don Fabrizio expects will succeed him, with the dog Benedico (who instinctively rejects Angelica) as a symbol of loyalty to the traditions of the past, moth-eaten and discarded by the end of the novel. Stanley G. Eskin, in his 1962 article in *Italica*, also investigates *The Leopard*'s extensive use of animal symbolism and relates it to Lampedusa's interest in the symbolist movement. Richard O'Mara, writing in the *Sewanee Review* in 2008, interprets the hyenas and jackals that the prince fears will succeed him as the Sicilian mafia, rather than the more usual reading as a reference to the Fascists, relating it to a more generalized or contemporary experience than to Lampedusa's own.

What Do I Read Next?

- *Letters from Londonand Europe* (2010, translated by J. G. Nichols) publishes recently discovered correspondence from Lampedusa to his relatives in Italy during the 1920s. The letters are similar to the introspective style and concerns of *The Leopard* and have much in common with nineteenth-century travel literature.

- G. A. Henty began his career as an officer in the British army during the Crimean War of the 1850s. His letters home about the awful conditions the British army suffered during the campaign because of the incompetence of senior officers (the publicizing of which also made Florence Nightingale famous) were published in newspapers and Henty soon found himself working as a war correspondent. One of the campaigns he covered was Garibaldi's invasion of Sicily and Naples, the historical backdrop of *The Leopard*. In his later career, Henty devoted himself to writing young-adult literature, producing nearly a hundred novels all set during various historical military campaigns ranging in time from ancient Egypt to the Franco-Prussian War of the early 1870s. In fact, Henty was one of the creators of the young-adult genre. In 1901 he published *Out with Garibaldi: A Story of the Liberation of Italy*, about the adventures of a half-English, halfItalian teenager who becomes one of Garibaldi's thousand, the volunteer corps with which he made his initial landing in Sicily. Readers should note that, like many Victorian authors, Henty was xenophobic (disliking foreigners) and imperialistic by modern standards.

- The four novels that make up Yukio Mis-hima's *Sea of Tranquility* tetralogy (*Spring Snow*, 1969; *Runaway Horses*, 1969; *The Temple of Dawn*, 1970; and *The Decay of the Angel*, 1971) are among the few works of world literature whose themes and attitude compare to those of *The Leopard*. The novels, set between 1912 and 1975, chronicle the decay of Japanese society over the course of the twentieth century through the eyes of a narrator who begins as a high school student and ends as a retired judge. In particular he narrates the lives of four young people he encounters over time who become more vicious and debased, without, nevertheless, losing an essential beauty, but whose lives all end in suicide. The first is his best friend from high school, and the narrator believes the other three are reincarnations of his friend.

- Gerard Gefen's *Sicily: Land of the Leopard Princes* (2001), with photographs by Jean-Bernard Naudin, offers an illustrated tour through the places described in *The Leopard*, supplemented by family photos of the Lampedusas.

- The collection of material by Lampedusa translated by Archibald Colquhoun in *Two Stories and a Memory* (1962) includes "Places of My Infancy," the memoir with which Lampedusa began the process of composing *The Leopard*, as well as two short stories that are his only other fiction.

- George Macaulay Trevelyan's 1911 *Garibaldi and the Making of Italy* is a classic account of the *Risorgimento*, especially in its military aspect, which is treated in minute detail.

Sources

Eskin, Stanley G., "Animal Imagery in *Il Gattopardo*," in *Italica*, Vol. 39, No. 3, 1962, pp. 189–94.

Evans, Arthur, and Catherine Evans, "'Salina e Svelto': The Symbolism of Change in *Il Gattopardo*," in *Wiscon-sin Studies in Contemporary Literature*, Vol. 4, No. 3, 1963, pp. 298–304.

Freud, Sigmund, *The Future of an Illusion*, translated and edited by James Strachey, W. W. Norton, 1961, pp. 5–71.

Gilmour, David, *The Last Leopard: A Life of Giuseppe di Lampedusa*, Pantheon Books, 1988, pp. 1–14, 188–89.

Lampedusa, Giuseppe Tomasi di, *The Leopard*, translated by Archibald Colquhoun, Pantheon Books, 1960.

Mercier, Vivian, "Sex, Success and Salvation," in *Hudson Review*, Vol. 13, No. 3, 1960, pp. 449–56.

O'Mara, Richard, "The Leopard Reconsidered," in *Sewanee Review*, Vol. 116, No. 4, 2008, pp. 637–44.

Sedgwick, Mark, *Against the Modern World: Traditionalism and the Secret Intellectual History of the Twentieth Century*, Oxford University Press, 2004, pp. 95–117.

Further Reading

Beales, Derek, and Eugenio Biagiani, *The Risorgimento and the Unification of Italy*, Longman, 2003.

> This is a standard textbook that deals with the historical and cultural aspects of the reunification of Italy.

Finley, Moses I., *A History of Sicily: Ancient Sicily to the Arab Conquest*, Viking, 1968.

> Although technically outdated, Finley's classic is elevated in style and literary significance far above an ordinary textbook. His evocation of the tragic history of the island brought comparisons to Lampedusa's *The Leopard* from reviewers.

Gefen, Gerard, *Sicilian Twilight: The Last Leopards*, Vendome, 2001.

> Gefen attempts to recreate the world of *The Leopard* with a combination of period documents and photographs as well as modern photos of the places described in the novel.

Moe, Nelson, *The View from Vesuvius: Italian Culture and the Southern Question*, University of California Press, 2002.

Moe discusses the current status of the integration of the former Kingdom of the Two Sicilies into the modern, unified Italian state.

Suggested Search Terms

Giuseppe Tomasi di Lampedusa

The Leopard

traditionalism

psychoanalysis

Julius Evola

Palermo

ancien régime

Freemasons